Works by Harold Pinter published by Grove Press

Complete Works: One (*The Birthday Party* • *The Room* • *The Dumb Waiter* •
A Slight Ache • *A Night Out* • "The Black and White" • "The Examination" •
"Writing for the Theatre")

Complete Works: Two (*The Caretaker* • *The Dwarfs* [play] • *The Collection* •
The Lover • *Night School* • *Trouble in the Works* • *The Black and White* •
Request Stop • *Last to Go* • *Special Offer* • "Writing for Myself")

Complete Works: Three (*The Homecoming* • *The Basement* • *Landscape* •
Silence • *Night* • *That's Your Trouble* • *That's All* • *Applicant* • *Interview* •
Dialogue for Three • *Tea Party* [play] • "Tea Party" [short story] • "Mac")

Complete Works: Four (*Old Times* • *No Man's Land* • *Betrayal* • *Monologue* •
Family Voices)

PLAYS AND SCREENPLAYS
Ashes to Ashes
Betrayal
The Birthday Party and The Room
The Caretaker and The Dumb Waiter
Five Screenplays (*The Servant* • *The Pumpkin Eater* •
    The Quiller Memorandum • *Accident* • *The Go-Between*)
The Homecoming
Moonlight
Mountain Language
No Man's Land
Old Times
One for the Road
Other Places: Three Plays (*A Kind of Alaska* • *Victoria Station* • *Family Voices*)
Party Time and The New World Order

POETRY AND PROSE
Collected Poems and Prose
The Dwarfs: A Novel
100 Poems by 100 Poets (an anthology selected by Harold Pinter, Geoffrey
    Godbert, and Anthony Astbury)
99 Poems in Translation (an anthology selected by Harold Pinter, Geoffrey
    Godbert, and Anthony Astbury)

THE HOMECOMING

THE HOMECOMING

Harold Pinter

GROVE PRESS
NEW YORK

Printed in the United States of America

Library of Congress Catalog Card Number 66-28734
ISBN 0-8021-5105-1

Grove Press
841 Broadway
New York, NY 10003

02   45 44 43 42 41 40

THE HOMECOMING was first presented by the Royal Shakespeare Company at the Aldwych Theatre on June 3, 1965, with the following cast:

MAX, *a man of seventy*	Paul Rogers
LENNY, *a man in his early thirties*	Ian Holm
SAM, *a man of sixty-three*	John Normington
JOEY, *a man in his middle twenties*	Terence Rigby
TEDDY, *a man in his middle thirties*	Michael Bryant
RUTH, *a woman in her early thirties*	Vivien Merchant

Directed by Peter Hall

The first American production opened at The Music Box on January 5, 1967. With the exception of the part of Teddy, which was played by Michael Craig, the cast was as above.

An old house in North London.

A large room, extending the width of the stage.

The back wall, which contained the door, has been removed. A square arch shape remains. Beyond it, the hall. In the hall a staircase, ascending U.L., well in view. The front door U.R. A coatstand, hooks, etc.

In the room a window, R. Odd tables, chairs. Two large armchairs. A large sofa, L. Against R. wall a large sideboard, the upper half of which contains a mirror. U.L., a radiogram.

Act One

Evening.

LENNY *is sitting on the sofa with a newspaper, a pencil in his hand. He wears a dark suit. He makes occasional marks on the back page.*

MAX *comes in, from the direction of the kitchen. He goes to sideboard, opens top drawer, rummages in it, closes it.*

He wears an old cardigan and a cap, and carries a stick.

He walks downstage, stands, looks about the room.

MAX. What have you done with the scissors?

Pause.

I said I'm looking for the scissors. What have you done with them?

Pause.

Did you hear me? I want to cut something out of the paper.

LENNY. I'm reading the paper.

MAX. Not that paper. I haven't even read that paper. I'm talking about last Sunday's paper. I was just having a look at it in the kitchen.

Pause.

Do you hear what I'm saying? I'm talking to you! Where's the scissors?

LENNY (*looking up, quietly*). Why don't you shut up, you daft prat?

MAX *lifts his stick and points it at him.*

MAX. Don't you talk to me like that. I'm warning you.

He sits in large armchair.

There's an advertisement in the paper about flannel vests. Cut price. Navy surplus. I could do with a few of them.

Pause.

I think I'll have a fag. Give me a fag.

Pause.

I just asked you to give me a cigarette.

Pause.

Look what I'm lumbered with.

He takes a crumpled cigarette from his pocket.

I'm getting old, my word of honour.

He lights it.

You think I wasn't a tearaway? I could have taken care of you, twice over. I'm still strong. You ask your Uncle Sam what I was. But at the same time I always had a kind heart. Always.

Pause.

I used to knock about with a man called MacGregor. I called him Mac. You remember Mac? Eh?

Pause.

Huhh! We were two of the worst hated men in the West End of London. I tell you, I still got the scars. We'd walk into a place, the whole room'd stand up, they'd make way to let us pass. You never heard such silence. Mind you, he was a big man, he was over six foot tall. His family were all MacGregors, they came all the way from Aberdeen, but he was the only one they called Mac.

Pause.

He was very fond of your mother, Mac was. Very fond. He always had a good word for her.

Pause.

Mind you, she wasn't such a bad woman. Even though it made me sick just to look at her rotten stinking face, she wasn't such a bad bitch. I gave her the best bleeding years of my life, anyway.

LENNY. Plug it, will you, you stupid sod, I'm trying to read the paper.

MAX. Listen! I'll chop your spine off, you talk to me like that! You understand? Talking to your lousy filthy father like that!

LENNY. You know what, you're getting demented.

Pause.

What do you think of Second Wind for the three-thirty?

MAX. Where?

LENNY. Sandown Park.

MAX. Don't stand a chance.

LENNY. Sure he does.

MAX. Not a chance.

LENNY. He's the winner.

LENNY *ticks the paper.*

MAX. He talks to me about horses.

Pause.

I used to live on the course. One of the loves of my life. Epsom? I knew it like the back of my hand. I was one of the best-known faces down at the paddock. What a marvellous open-air life.

Pause.

He talks to me about horses. You only read their names in the papers. But I've stroked their manes, I've held them, I've calmed them down before a big race. I was the one they used to call for. Max, they'd say, there's a horse here, he's highly strung, you're the only man on the course who can calm him. It was true. I had a . . . I had an instinctive understanding of animals. I should have been a trainer. Many times I was offered the job – you know, a proper post, by the Duke of . . . I forget his name . . . one of the Dukes. But I had family obligations, my family needed me at home.

Pause.

The times I've watched those animals thundering past the post. What an experience. Mind you, I didn't lose, I made a few bob out of it, and you know why? Because I always had the smell of a good horse. I could smell him. And not only the colts but the fillies. Because the fillies are more highly strung than the colts, they're more unreliable, did you know that? No, what do you know? Nothing. But I was always able to tell a good filly by one particular trick. I'd look her in the eye. You see? I'd stand in front of her and look her straight in the eye, it was a kind of hypnotism, and by the look deep down in her eye I could tell whether she was a stayer or not. It was a gift. I had a gift.

Pause.

And he talks to me about horses.

LENNY. Dad, do you mind if I change the subject?

Pause.

I want to ask you something. That dinner we had before, what was the name of it? What do you call it?

Pause.

Why don't you buy a dog? You're a dog cook. Honest. You think you're cooking for a lot of dogs.

MAX. If you don't like it get out.

LENNY. I am going out. I'm going out to buy myself a proper dinner.

MAX. Well, get out! What are you waiting for?

LENNY *looks at him.*

LENNY. What did you say?

MAX. I said shove off out of it, that's what I said.

LENNY. You'll go before me, Dad, if you talk to me in that tone of voice.

MAX. Will I, you bitch?

MAX *grips his stick.*

LENNY. Oh, Daddy, you're not going to use your stick on me, are you? Eh? Don't use your stick on me, Daddy. No, please. It wasn't my fault, it was one of the others. I haven't done anything wrong, Dad, honest. Don't clout me with that stick, Dad.

Silence.

MAX *sits hunched.* LENNY *reads the paper.*

SAM *comes in the front door. He wears a chauffeur's uniform. He hangs his hat on a hook in the hall and comes into the room. He goes to a chair, sits in it and sighs.*

Hullo, Uncle Sam.

SAM. Hullo.

LENNY. How are you, Uncle?

SAM. Not bad. A bit tired.

LENNY. Tired? I bet you're tired. Where you been?

SAM. I've been to London Airport.

LENNY. All the way up to London Airport? What, right up the M4?

SAM. Yes, all the way up there.

LENNY. Tch, tch, tch. Well, I think you're entitled to be tired, Uncle.

SAM. Well, it's the drivers.

LENNY. I know. That's what I'm talking about. I'm talking about the drivers.

SAM. Knocks you out.

Pause.

MAX. I'm here, too, you know.

SAM *looks at him.*

I said I'm here, too. I'm sitting here.

SAM. I know you're here.

Pause.

SAM. I took a Yankee out there today . . . to the Airport.

LENNY. Oh, a Yankee, was it?

SAM. Yes, I been with him all day. Picked him up at the Savoy at half past twelve, took him to the Caprice for his lunch. After lunch I picked him up again, took him down to a house in Eaton Square – he had to pay a visit to a friend there – and then round about tea-time I took him right the way out to the Airport.

LENNY. Had to catch a plane there, did he?

SAM. Yes. Look what he gave me. He gave me a box of cigars.

SAM *takes a box of cigars from his pocket.*

MAX. Come here. Let's have a look at them.

SAM *shows* MAX *the cigars.* MAX *takes one from the box, pinches it and sniffs it.*

It's a fair cigar.

SAM. Want to try one?

MAX *and* SAM *light cigars.*

You know what he said to me? He told me I was the best chauffeur he'd ever had. The best one.

MAX. From what point of view?

SAM. Eh?

MAX. From what point of view?

LENNY. From the point of view of his driving, Dad, and his general sense of courtesy, I should say.

MAX. Thought you were a good driver, did he, Sam? Well, he gave you a first-class cigar.

SAM. Yes, he thought I was the best he'd ever had. They all say that, you know. They won't have anyone else, they only ask for me. They say I'm the best chauffeur in the firm.

LENNY. I bet the other drivers tend to get jealous, don't they, Uncle?

SAM. They do get jealous. They get very jealous.

MAX. Why?

Pause.

SAM. I just told you.

MAX. No, I just can't get it clear, Sam. Why do the other drivers get jealous?

SAM. Because (a) I'm the best driver, and because . . . (b) I don't take liberties.

Pause.

I don't press myself on people, you see. These big businessmen, men of affairs, they don't want the driver jawing all the time, they like to sit in the back, have a bit of peace and quiet. After all, they're sitting in a Humber Super Snipe, they can afford to relax. At the same time, though, this is what really makes me special . . . I do know how to pass the time of day when required.

Pause.

For instance, I told this man today I was in the second world war. Not the first. I told him I was too young for the first. But I told him I fought in the second.

Pause.

So did he, it turned out.

LENNY *stands, goes to the mirror and straightens his tie.*

LENNY. He was probably a colonel, or something, in the American Air Force.

SAM. Yes.

LENNY. Probably a navigator, or something like that, in a Flying Fortress. Now he's most likely a high executive in a worldwide group of aeronautical engineers.

SAM. Yes.

LENNY. Yes, I know the kind of man you're talking about.

LENNY *goes out, turning to his right.*

SAM. After all, I'm experienced. I was driving a dust cart at the age of nineteen. Then I was in long-distance haulage. I had ten years as a taxi-driver and I've had five as a private chauffeur.

MAX. It's funny you never got married, isn't it? A man with all your gifts.

Pause.

Isn't it? A man like you?

SAM. There's still time.

MAX. Is there?

Pause.

SAM. You'd be surprised.

MAX. What you been doing, banging away at your lady customers, have you?

SAM. Not me.

MAX. In the back of the Snipe? Been having a few crafty reefs in a layby, have you?

SAM. Not me.

MAX. On the back seat? What about the armrest, was it up or down?

SAM. I've never done that kind of thing in my car.

MAX. Above all that kind of thing, are you, Sam?

SAM. Too true.

MAX. Above having a good bang on the back seat, are you?

SAM. Yes, I leave that to others.

MAX. You leave it to others? What others? You paralysed prat!

SAM. I don't mess up my car! Or my . . . my boss's car! Like other people.

MAX. Other people? What other people?

Pause.

What other people?

Pause.

SAM. Other people.

Pause.

MAX. When you find the right girl, Sam, let your family know, don't forget, we'll give you a number one send-off, I promise you. You can bring her to live here, she can keep us all happy. We'd take it in turns to give her a walk round the park.

SAM. I wouldn't bring her here.

MAX. Sam, it's your decision. You're welcome to bring your bride here, to the place where you live, or on the other hand you can take a suite at the Dorchester. It's entirely up to you.

SAM. I haven't got a bride.

SAM stands, goes to the sideboard, takes an apple from the bowl, bites into it.

Getting a bit peckish.

He looks out of the window.

Never get a bride like you had, anyway. Nothing like your bride . . . going about these days. Like Jessie.

Pause.

After all, I escorted her once or twice, didn't I? Drove her round once or twice in my cab. She was a charming woman.

Pause.

All the same, she was your wife. But still . . . they were some of the most delightful evenings I've ever had. Used to just drive her about. It was my pleasure.

MAX (*softly, closing his eyes*). Christ.

SAM. I used to pull up at a stall and buy her a cup of coffee. She was a very nice companion to be with.

Silence.
JOEY comes in the front door. He walks into the room, takes his jacket off, throws it on a chair and stands.
Silence.

JOEY. Feel a bit hungry.

SAM. Me, too.

MAX. Who do you think I am, your mother? Eh? Honest. They walk in here every time of the day and night like bloody animals. Go and find yourself a mother.

LENNY walks into the room, stands.

JOEY. I've been training down at the gym.

SAM. Yes, the boy's been working all day and training all night.

MAX. What do you want, you bitch? You spend all the day sitting on your arse at London Airport, buy yourself a jamroll. You expect me to sit here waiting to rush into the kitchen the moment you step in the door? You've been living sixty-three years, why don't you learn to cook?

SAM. I can cook.

MAX. Well, go and cook!

Pause.

LENNY. What the boys want, Dad, is your own special brand of cooking, Dad. That's what the boys look forward to. The special understanding of food, you know, that you've got.

MAX. Stop calling me Dad. Just stop all that calling me Dad, do you understand?

LENNY. But I'm your son. You used to tuck me up in bed every night. He tucked you up, too, didn't he, Joey?

Pause.

He used to like tucking up his sons.

LENNY *turns and goes towards the front door.*

MAX. Lenny.

LENNY (*turning*). What?

MAX. I'll give you a proper tuck up one of these nights, son. You mark my word.

They look at each other.
LENNY *opens the front door and goes out.*
Silence.

JOEY. I've been training with Bobby Dodd.

Pause.

And I had a good go at the bag as well.

Pause.

I wasn't in bad trim.

MAX. Boxing's a gentleman's game.

Pause.

I'll tell you what you've got to do. What you've got to do is you've got to learn how to defend yourself, and you've got to learn how to attack. That's your only trouble as a boxer. You don't know how to defend yourself, and you don't know how to attack.

Pause.

Once you've mastered those arts you can go straight to the top.

Pause.

JOEY. I've got a pretty good idea . . . of how to do that.

JOEY *looks round for his jacket, picks it up, goes out of the room and up the stairs.*
Pause.

MAX. Sam . . . why don't you go, too, eh? Why don't you just go upstairs? Leave me quiet. Leave me alone.

SAM. I want to make something clear about Jessie, Max. I want to. I do. When I took her out in the cab, round the town, I was taking care of her, for you. I was looking after her for you, when you were busy, wasn't I? I was showing her the West End.

Pause.

You wouldn't have trusted any of your other brothers. You wouldn't have trusted Mac, would you? But you trusted me. I want to remind you.

Pause.

Old Mac died a few years ago, didn't he? Isn't he dead?

Pause.

He was a lousy stinking rotten loudmouth. A bastard uncouth sodding runt. Mind you, he was a good friend of yours.

Pause.

MAX. Eh, Sam . . .
SAM. What?
MAX. Why do I keep you here? You're just an old grub.

SAM. Am I?

MAX. You're a maggot.

SAM. Oh yes?

MAX. As soon as you stop paying your way here, I mean when you're too old to pay your way, you know what I'm going to do? I'm going to give you the boot.

SAM. You are, eh?

MAX. Sure. I mean, bring in the money and I'll put up with you. But when the firm gets rid of you – you can flake off.

SAM. This is my house as well, you know. This was our mother's house.

MAX. One lot after the other. One mess after the other.

SAM. Our father's house.

MAX. Look what I'm lumbered with. One cast-iron bunch of crap after another. One flow of stinking pus after another.

Pause.

Our father? I remember him. Don't worry. You kid yourself. He used to come over to me and look down at me. My old man did. He'd bend right over me, then he'd pick me up. I was only that big. Then he'd dandle me. Give me the bottle. Wipe me clean. Give me a smile. Pat me on the bum. Pass me around, pass me from hand to hand. Toss me up in the air. Catch me coming down. I remember my father.

BLACKOUT.
LIGHTS UP.
Night.
TEDDY *and* RUTH *stand at the threshold of the room.*
They are both well dressed in light summer suits and light raincoats.
Two suitcases are by their side.
They look at the room. TEDDY *tosses the key in his hand,*
smiles.

TEDDY. Well, the key worked.

Pause.

They haven't changed the lock.

Pause.

RUTH. No one's here.
TEDDY (*looking up*). They're asleep.

Pause.

RUTH. Can I sit down?
TEDDY. Of course.
RUTH. I'm tired.

Pause.

TEDDY. Then sit down.

She does not move.

That's my father's chair.
RUTH. That one?
TEDDY (*smiling*). Yes, that's it. Shall I go up and see if my room's still there?
RUTH. It can't have moved.
TEDDY. No, I mean if my bed's still there.
RUTH. Someone might be in it.
TEDDY. No. They've got their own beds.

Pause.

RUTH. Shouldn't you wake someone up? Tell them you're here?
TEDDY. Not at this time of night. It's too late.

Pause.

Shall I go up?

He goes into the hall, looks up the stairs, comes bacк.

Why don't you sit down?

Pause.

I'll just go up . . . have a look.

He goes up the stairs, stealthily.
RUTH *stands, then slowly walks across the room.*
TEDDY *returns.*

It's still there. My room. Empty. The bed's there. What are you doing?

She looks at him.

Blankets, no sheets. I'll find some sheets. I could hear snores. Really. They're all still here, I think. They're all snoring up there. Are you cold?

RUTH. No.

TEDDY. I'll make something to drink, if you like. Something hot.

RUTH. No, I don't want anything.

TEDDY *walks about.*

TEDDY. What do you think of the room? Big, isn't it? It's a big house. I mean, it's a fine room, don't you think? Actually there was a wall, across there . . . with a door. We knocked it down . . . years ago . . . to make an open living area. The structure wasn't affected, you see. My mother was dead.

RUTH *sits.*

Tired?

RUTH. Just a little.

TEDDY. We can go to bed if you like. No point in waking anyone up now. Just go to bed. See them all in the morning . . . see my father in the morning. . . .

Pause.

RUTH. Do you want to stay?

TEDDY. Stay?

Pause.

We've come to stay. We're bound to stay . . . for a few
days.

RUTH. I think . . . the children . . . might be missing us.

TEDDY. Don't be silly.

RUTH. They might.

TEDDY. Look, we'll be back in a few days, won't we?

He walks about the room.

Nothing's changed. Still the same.

Pause.

Still, he'll get a surprise in the morning, won't he? The old
man. I think you'll like him very much. Honestly. He's a
. . . well, he's old, of course. Getting on.

Pause.

I was born here, do you realize that?

RUTH. I know.

Pause.

TEDDY. Why don't you go to bed? I'll find some sheets. I
feel . . . wide awake, isn't it odd? I think I'll stay up for
a bit. Are you tired?

RUTH. No.

TEDDY. Go to bed. I'll show you the room.

RUTH. No, I don't want to.

TEDDY. You'll be perfectly all right up there without me.
Really you will. I mean, I won't be long. Look, it's just up
there. It's the first door on the landing. The bathroom's
right next door. You . . . need some rest, you know.

Pause.

I just want to . . . walk about for a few minutes. Do you mind?

RUTH. Of course I don't.

TEDDY. Well . . . Shall I show you the room?

RUTH. No, I'm happy at the moment.

TEDDY. You don't have to go to bed. I'm not saying you have to. I mean, you can stay up with me. Perhaps I'll make a cup of tea or something. The only thing is we don't want to make too much noise, we don't want to wake anyone up.

RUTH. I'm not making any noise.

TEDDY. I know you're not.

He goes to her.

(*Gently.*) Look, it's all right, really. I'm here. I mean . . . I'm with you. There's no need to be nervous. Are you nervous?

RUTH. No.

TEDDY. There's no need to be.

Pause.

They're very warm people, really. Very warm. They're my family. They're not ogres.

Pause.

Well, perhaps we should go to bed. After all, we have to be up early, see Dad. Wouldn't be quite right if he found us in bed, I think. (*He chuckles.*) Have to be up before six, come down, say hullo.

Pause.

RUTH. I think I'll have a breath of air.

TEDDY. Air?

Pause.

What do you mean?

RUTH (*standing*). Just a stroll.

TEDDY. At this time of night? But we've . . . only just got here. We've got to go to bed.

RUTH. I just feel like some air.

TEDDY. But I'm going to bed.

RUTH. That's all right.

TEDDY. But what am I going to do?

Pause.

The last thing I want is a breath of air. Why do you want a breath of air?

RUTH. I just do.

TEDDY. But it's late.

RUTH. I won't go far. I'll come back.

Pause.

TEDDY. I'll wait up for you.

RUTH. Why?

TEDDY. I'm not going to bed without you.

RUTH. Can I have the key?

He gives it to her.

Why don't you go to bed?

He puts his arms on her shoulders and kisses her.
They look at each other, briefly. She smiles.

I won't be long.

She goes out of the front door.
TEDDY goes to the window, peers out after her, half turns from the window, stands, suddenly chews his knuckles.
LENNY walks into the room from U.L. He stands. He wears pyjamas and dressing-gown. He watches TEDDY.
TEDDY turns and sees him.
Silence.

TEDDY. Hullo, Lenny.
LENNY. Hullo, Teddy.

Pause.

TEDDY. I didn't hear you come down the stairs.
LENNY. I didn't.

Pause.

I sleep down here now. Next door. I've got a kind of study, workroom cum bedroom next door now, you see.
TEDDY. Oh. Did I . . . wake you up?
LENNY. No. I just had an early night tonight. You know how it is. Can't sleep. Keep waking up.

Pause.

TEDDY. How are you?
LENNY. Well, just sleeping a bit restlessly, that's all. Tonight, anyway.
TEDDY. Bad dreams?
LENNY. No, I wouldn't say I was dreaming. It's not exactly a dream. It's just that something keeps waking me up. Some kind of tick.
TEDDY. A tick?
LENNY. Yes.
TEDDY. Well, what is it?
LENNY. I don't know.

Pause.

TEDDY. Have you got a clock in your room?
LENNY. Yes.
TEDDY. Well, maybe it's the clock.
LENNY. Yes, could be, I suppose.

Pause.

Well, if it's the clock I'd better do something about it. Stifle it in some way, or something.

Pause.

TEDDY. I've . . . just come back for a few days.
LENNY. Oh yes? Have you?

Pause.

TEDDY. How's the old man?
LENNY. He's in the pink.

Pause.

TEDDY. I've been keeping well.
LENNY. Oh, have you?

Pause.

Staying the night then, are you?
TEDDY. Yes.
LENNY. Well, you can sleep in your old room.
TEDDY. Yes, I've been up.
LENNY. Yes, you can sleep there.

LENNY *yawns.*

Oh well.
TEDDY. I'm going to bed.
LENNY. Are you?
TEDDY. Yes, I'll get some sleep.
LENNY. Yes, I'm going to bed, too.

TEDDY *picks up the cases.*

I'll give you a hand.
TEDDY. No, they're not heavy.

TEDDY *goes into the hall with the cases.*
LENNY *turns out the light in the room.*
The light in the hall remains on.
LENNY *follows into the hall.*

LENNY. Nothing you want?

TEDDY. Mmmm?

LENNY. Nothing you might want, for the night? Glass of water, anything like that?

TEDDY. Any sheets anywhere?

LENNY. In the sideboard in your room.

TEDDY. Oh, good.

LENNY. Friends of mine occasionally stay there, you know, in your room, when they're passing through this part of the world.

> LENNY *turns out the hall light and turns on the first landing light.*
> TEDDY *begins to walk up the stairs.*

TEDDY. Well, I'll see you at breakfast, then.

LENNY. Yes, that's it. Ta-ta.

> TEDDY *goes upstairs.*
> LENNY *goes off* L.
> *Silence.*
> *The landing light goes out.*
> *Slight night light in the hall and room.*
> LENNY *comes back into the room, goes to the window and looks out.*
> *He leaves the window and turns on a lamp.*
> *He is holding a small clock.*
> *He sits, places the clock in front of him, lights a cigarette and sits.*
> RUTH *comes in the front door.*
> *She stands still.* LENNY *turns his head, smiles. She walks slowly into the room.*

LENNY. Good evening.

RUTH. Morning, I think.

LENNY. You're right there.

> *Pause.*

My name's Lenny. What's yours?

RUTH. Ruth.

She sits, puts her coat collar around her.

LENNY. Cold?
RUTH. No.
LENNY. It's been a wonderful summer, hasn't it? Remarkable.

   Pause.

Would you like something? Refreshment of some kind? An aperitif, anything like that?
RUTH. No, thanks.
LENNY. I'm glad you said that. We haven't got a drink in the house. Mind you, I'd soon get some in, if we had a party or something like that. Some kind of celebration . . . you know.

   Pause.

You must be connected with my brother in some way. The one who's been abroad.
RUTH. I'm his wife.
LENNY. Eh listen, I wonder if you can advise me. I've been having a bit of a rough time with this clock. The tick's been keeping me up. The trouble is I'm not all that convinced it was the clock. I mean there are lots of things which tick in the night, don't you find that? All sorts of objects, which, in the day, you wouldn't call anything else but commonplace. They give you no trouble. But in the night any given one of a number of them is liable to start letting out a bit of a tick. Whereas you look at these objects in the day and they're just commonplace. They're as quiet as mice during the daytime. So . . . all things being equal . . . this question of me saying it was the clock that woke me up, well, that could very easily prove something of a false hypothesis.

He goes to the sideboard, pours from a jug into a glass, takes the glass to RUTH.

Here you are. I bet you could do with this.

RUTH. What is it?

LENNY. Water.

She takes it, sips, places the glass on a small table by her chair.

LENNY *watches her.*

Isn't it funny? I've got my pyjamas on and you're fully dressed?

He goes to the sideboard and pours another glass of water.

Mind if I have one? Yes, it's funny seeing my old brother again after all these years. It's just the sort of tonic my Dad needs, you know. He'll be chuffed to his bollocks in the morning, when he sees his eldest son. I was surprised myself when I saw Teddy, you know. Old Ted. I thought he was in America.

RUTH. We're on a visit to Europe.

LENNY. What, both of you?

RUTH. Yes.

LENNY. What, you sort of live with him over there, do you?

RUTH. We're married.

LENNY. On a visit to Europe, eh? Seen much of it?

RUTH. We've just come from Italy.

LENNY. Oh, you went to Italy first, did you? And then he brought you over here to meet the family, did he? Well, the old man'll be pleased to see you, I can tell you.

RUTH. Good.

LENNY. What did you say?

RUTH. Good.

Pause.

LENNY. Where'd you go to in Italy?

RUTH. Venice.

LENNY. Not dear old Venice? Eh? That's funny. You know, I've always had a feeling that if I'd been a soldier in the last war – say in the Italian campaign – I'd probably have found myself in Venice. I've always had that feeling. The trouble was I was too young to serve, you see. I was only a child, I was too small, otherwise I've got a pretty shrewd idea I'd probably have gone through Venice. Yes, I'd almost certainly have gone through it with my battalion. Do you mind if I hold your hand?

RUTH. Why?

LENNY. Just a touch.

He stands and goes to her.

Just a tickle.

RUTH. Why?

He looks down at her.

LENNY. I'll tell you why.

Slight pause.

One night, not too long ago, one night down by the docks, I was standing alone under an arch, watching all the men jibbing the boom, out in the harbour, and playing about with the yardarm, when a certain lady came up to me and made me a certain proposal. This lady had been searching for me for days. She'd lost track of my whereabouts. However, the fact was she eventually caught up with me, and when she caught up with me she made me this certain proposal. Well, this proposal wasn't entirely out of order and normally I would have subscribed to it. I mean I would have subscribed to it in the normal course of events. The only trouble was she was falling apart with the pox. So I turned it down. Well, this lady was very insistent and started taking liberties with me down under this arch, liberties which by any criterion I couldn't be expected to tolerate, the facts being what they were, so I clumped her one. It was on my mind at the time to do away with her, you know, to kill her, and the fact is, that as killings go, it would have been a simple matter, nothing to it. Her chauffeur, who had located me for her, he'd popped round the corner to have a drink, which just left this lady and myself, you see, alone, standing underneath this arch, watching all the steamers steaming up, no one about, all quiet on the Western Front, and there she was up against this wall – well, just sliding down the wall, following the blow I'd given her. Well, to sum up, everything was in my favour, for a killing. Don't worry about the chauffeur. The chauffeur would never have spoken. He was an old friend of the family. But . . . in the end I thought . . . Aaah, why go to all the bother . . . you know, getting rid of the corpse and all that, getting yourself into a state of tension. So I just gave her another belt in the nose and a couple of turns of the boot and sort of left it at that.

RUTH. How did you know she was diseased?
LENNY. How did I know?

Pause.

I decided she was.

Silence.

You and my brother are newly-weds, are you?
RUTH. We've been married six years.
LENNY. He's always been my favourite brother, old Teddy. Do you know that? And my goodness we are proud of him here, I can tell you. Doctor of Philosophy and all that . . . leaves quite an impression. Of course, he's a very sensitive man, isn't he? Ted. Very. I've often wished I was as sensitive as he is.
RUTH. Have you?

LENNY. Oh yes. Oh yes, very much so. I mean, I'm not saying I'm not sensitive. I am. I could just be a bit more so, that's all.

RUTH. Could you?

LENNY. Yes, just a bit more so, that's all.

Pause.

I mean, I am very sensitive to atmosphere, but I tend to get desensitized, if you know what I mean, when people make unreasonable demands on me. For instance, last Christmas I decided to do a bit of snow-clearing for the Borough Council, because we had a heavy snow over here that year in Europe. I didn't have to do this snow-clearing – I mean I wasn't financially embarrassed in any way – it just appealed to me, it appealed to something inside me. What I anticipated with a good deal of pleasure was the brisk cold bite in the air in the early morning. And I was right. I had to get my snowboots on and I had to stand on a corner, at about five-thirty in the morning, to wait for the lorry to pick me up, to take me to the allotted area. Bloody freezing. Well, the lorry came, I jumped on the tailboard, headlights on, dipped, and off we went. Got there, shovels up, fags on, and off we went, deep into the December snow, hours before cockcrow. Well, that morning, while I was having my mid-morning cup of tea in a neighbouring cafe, the shovel standing by my chair, an old lady approached me and asked me if I would give her a hand with her iron mangle. Her brother-in-law, she said, had left it for her, but he'd left it in the wrong room, he'd left it in the front room. Well, naturally, she wanted it in the back room. It was a present he'd given her, you see, a mangle, to iron out the washing. But he'd left it in the wrong room, he'd left it in the front room, well that was a silly place to leave it, it couldn't stay there. So I took time off to give her a hand. She only lived up the road. Well, the only trouble was when I got there I couldn't move this mangle. It must have weighed about half a ton. How this brother-in-law got it up there in the first place I can't even begin to envisage. So there I was, doing a bit of shoulders on with the mangle, risking a rupture, and this old lady just standing there, waving me on, not even lifting a little finger to give me a helping hand. So after a few minutes I said to her, now look here, why don't you stuff this iron mangle up your arse? Anyway, I said, they're out of date, you want to get a spin drier. I had a good mind to give her a workover there and then, but as I was feeling jubilant with the snow-clearing I just gave her a short-arm jab to the belly and jumped on a bus outside. Excuse me, shall I take this ashtray out of your way?

RUTH. It's not in my way.

LENNY. It seems to be in the way of your glass. The glass was about to fall. Or the ashtray. I'm rather worried about the carpet. It's not me, it's my father. He's obsessed with order and clarity. He doesn't like mess. So, as I don't believe you're smoking at the moment, I'm sure you won't object if I move the ashtray.

He does so.

And now perhaps I'll relieve you of your glass.

RUTH. I haven't quite finished.

LENNY. You've consumed quite enough, in my opinion.

RUTH. No, I haven't.

LENNY. Quite sufficient, in my own opinion.

RUTH. Not in mine, Leonard.

Pause.

LENNY. Don't call me that, please.

RUTH. Why not?

LENNY. That's the name my mother gave me.

Pause.

Just give me the glass.

RUTH. No.

Pause.

LENNY. I'll take it, then.

RUTH. If you take the glass . . . I'll take you.

Pause.

LENNY. How about me taking the glass without you taking me?

RUTH. Why don't I just take you?

Pause.

LENNY. You're joking.

Pause.

You're in love, anyway, with another man. You've had a secret liaison with another man. His family didn't even know. Then you come here without a word of warning and start to make trouble.

She picks up the glass and lifts it towards him.

RUTH. Have a sip. Go on. Have a sip from my glass.

He is still.

Sit on my lap. Take a long cool sip.

She pats her lap. Pause.
She stands, moves to him with the glass.

Put your head back and open your mouth.

LENNY. Take that glass away from me.

RUTH. Lie on the floor. Go on. I'll pour it down your throat.

LENNY. What are you doing, making me some kind of proposal?

She laughs shortly, drains the glass.

RUTH. Oh, I was thirsty.

She smiles at him, puts the glass down, goes into the hall and up the stairs.
He follows into the hall and shouts up the stairs.

LENNY. What was that supposed to be? Some kind of proposal?

Silence.
He comes back into the room, goes to his own glass, drains it.
A door slams upstairs.
The landing light goes on.
MAX *comes down the stairs, in pyjamas and cap. He comes into the room.*

MAX. What's going on here? You drunk?

He stares at LENNY.

What are you shouting about? You gone mad?

LENNY *pours another glass of water.*

Prancing about in the middle of the night shouting your
head off. What are you, a raving lunatic?
LENNY. I was thinking aloud.
MAX. Is Joey down here? You been shouting at Joey?
LENNY. Didn't you hear what I said, Dad? I said I was
thinking aloud.
MAX. You were thinking so loud you got me out of bed.
LENNY. Look, why don't you just . . . pop off, eh?
MAX. Pop off? He wakes me up in the middle of the night, I
think we got burglars here, I think he's got a knife stuck in
him, I come down here, he tells me to pop off.

LENNY *sits down.*

He was talking to someone. Who could he have been talking
to? They're all asleep. He was having a conversation with

someone. He won't tell me who it was. He pretends he was thinking aloud. What are you doing, hiding someone here?

LENNY. I was sleepwalking. Get out of it, leave me alone, will you?

MAX. I want an explanation, you understand? I asked you who you got hiding here.

Pause.

LENNY. I'll tell you what, Dad, since you're in the mood for a bit of a . . . chat, I'll ask you a question. It's a question I've been meaning to ask you for some time. That night . . . you know . . . the night you got me . . . that night with Mum, what was it like? Eh? When I was just a glint in your eye. What was it like? What was the background to it? I mean, I want to know the real facts about my background. I mean, for instance, is it a fact that you had me in mind all the time, or is it a fact that I was the last thing you had in mind?

Pause.

I'm only asking this in a spirit of inquiry, you understand that, don't you? I'm curious. And there's lots of people of my age share that curiosity, you know that, Dad? They often ruminate, sometimes singly, sometimes in groups, about the true facts of that particular night—the night they were made in the image of those two people *at it*. It's a question long overdue, from my point of view, but as we happen to be passing the time of day here tonight I thought I'd pop it to you.

Pause.

MAX. You'll drown in your own blood.

LENNY. If you prefer to answer the question in writing I've got no objection.

MAX *stands.*

I should have asked my dear mother. Why didn't I ask my dear mother? Now it's too late. She's passed over to the other side.

MAX *spits at him.*
LENNY *looks down at the carpet.*

Now look what you've done. I'll have to Hoover that in the morning, you know.

MAX *turns and walks up the stairs.*
LENNY *sits still.*
BLACKOUT.
LIGHTS UP.

Morning.
JOEY *in front of the mirror. He is doing some slow limbering-up exercises. He stops, combs his hair, carefully. He then shadowboxes, heavily, watching himself in the mirror.*
MAX *comes in from* U.L.
Both MAX *and* JOEY *are dressed.* MAX *watches* JOEY *in silence.* JOEY *stops shadowboxing, picks up a newspaper and sits.*
Silence.

MAX. I hate this room.

Pause.

It's the kitchen I like. It's nice in there. It's cosy.

Pause.

But I can't stay in there. You know why? Because he's always washing up in there, scraping the plates, driving me out of the kitchen, that's why.
JOEY. Why don't you bring your tea in here?
MAX. I don't want to bring my tea in here. I hate it here. I want to drink my tea in there.

He goes into the hall and looks towards the kitchen.

What's he doing in there?

He returns.

What's the time?
JOEY. Half past six.
MAX. Half past six.

Pause.

I'm going to see a game of football this afternoon. You want to come?

Pause.

I'm talking to you.
JOEY. I'm training this afternoon. I'm doing six rounds with Blackie.
MAX. That's not till five o'clock. You've got time to see a game of football before five o'clock. It's the first game of the season.
JOEY. No, I'm not going.
MAX. Why not?

Pause.
MAX *goes into the hall.*

Sam! Come here!

MAX comes back into the room.
SAM enters with a cloth.

SAM. What?
MAX. What are you doing in there?
SAM. Washing up.
MAX. What else?
SAM. Getting rid of your leavings.
MAX. Putting them in the bin, eh?

SAM. Right in.

MAX. What point you trying to prove?

SAM. No point.

MAX. Oh yes, you are. You resent making my breakfast, that's what it is, isn't it? That's why you bang round the kitchen like that, scraping the frying-pan, scraping all the leavings into the bin, scraping all the plates, scraping all the tea out of the teapot . . . that's why you do that, every single stinking morning. I know. Listen, Sam. I want to say something to you. From my heart.

He moves closer.

I want you to get rid of these feelings of resentment you've got towards me. I wish I could understand them. Honestly, have I ever given you cause? Never. When Dad died he said to me, Max, look after your brothers. That's exactly what he said to me.

SAM. How could he say that when he was dead?

MAX. What?

SAM. How could he speak if he was dead?

Pause.

MAX. Before he died, Sam. Just before. They were his last words. His last sacred words, Sammy. A split second after he said those words . . . he was a dead man. You think I'm joking? You think when my father spoke – on his death-bed – I wouldn't obey his words to the last letter? You hear that, Joey? He'll stop at nothing. He's even prepared to spit on the memory of our Dad. What kind of a son were you, you wet wick? You spent half your time doing crossword puzzles! We took you into the butcher's shop, you couldn't even sweep the dust off the floor. We took MacGregor into the shop, he could run the place by the end of a week. Well, I'll tell you one thing. I respected my father not only as a man but as a number one butcher! And to prove it I followed him into the shop. I learned to carve a carcass at his knee. I commemorated his name in blood. I gave birth to three grown men! All on my own bat. What have you done?

Pause.

What have you done? You tit!

SAM. Do you want to finish the washing up? Look, here's the cloth.

MAX. So try to get rid of these feelings of resentment, Sam. After all, we are brothers.

SAM. Do you want the cloth? Here you are. Take it.

> TEDDY *and* RUTH *come down the stairs. They walk across the hall and stop just inside the room.*
> *The others turn and look at them.* JOEY *stands.*
> TEDDY *and* RUTH *are wearing dressing-gowns.*
> *Silence.*
> TEDDY *smiles.*

TEDDY. Hullo . . . Dad . . . We overslept.

Pause.

What's for breakfast?

> *Silence.*
> TEDDY *chuckles.*

Huh. We overslept.

> MAX *turns to* SAM.

MAX. Did you know he was here?

SAM. No.

> MAX *turns to* JOEY.

MAX. Did you know he was here?

Pause.

I asked you if you knew he was here.
JOEY. No.
MAX. Then who knew?

Pause.

Who knew?

Pause.

I didn't know.
TEDDY. I was going to come down, Dad, I was going to . . .
be here, when you came down.

Pause.

How are you?

Pause.

Uh . . . look, I'd . . . like you to meet . . .
MAX. How long you been in this house?
TEDDY. All night.
MAX. All night? I'm a laughing-stock. How did you get in?
TEDDY. I had my key.

MAX *whistles and laughs.*

MAX. Who's this?
TEDDY. I was just going to introduce you.
MAX. Who asked you to bring tarts in here?
TEDDY. Tarts?
MAX. Who asked you to bring dirty tarts into this house?
TEDDY. Listen, don't be silly—
MAX. You been here all night?
TEDDY. Yes, we arrived from Venice—
MAX. We've had a smelly scrubber in my house all night.
   We've had a stinking pox-ridden slut in my house all night.

TEDDY. Stop it! What are you talking about?

MAX. I haven't seen the bitch for six years, he comes home without a word, he brings a filthy scrubber off the street, he shacks up in my house!

TEDDY. She's my wife! We're married!

Pause.

MAX. I've never had a whore under this roof before. Ever since your mother died. My word of honour. (*To* JOEY.) Have you ever had a whore here? Has Lenny ever had a whore here? They come back from America, they bring the slopbucket with them. They bring the bedpan with them. (*To* TEDDY.) Take that disease away from me. Get her away from me.

TEDDY. She's my wife.

MAX (*to* JOEY). Chuck them out.

Pause.

A Doctor of Philosophy. Sam, you want to meet a Doctor of Philosophy? (*To* JOEY.) I said chuck them out.

Pause.

What's the matter? You deaf?

JOEY. You're an old man. (*To* TEDDY.) He's an old man.

LENNY *walks into the room, in a dressing-gown.*
He stops.
They all look round.
MAX *turns back, hits* JOEY *in the stomach with all his might.*
JOEY *contorts, staggers across the stage.* MAX, *with the exertion of the blow, begins to collapse. His knees buckle. He clutches his stick.*
SAM *moves forward to help him.*
MAX *hits him across the head with his stick.* SAM *sits, head in hands.*

JOEY, *hands pressed to his stomach, sinks down at the feet of*
RUTH.
She looks down at him.
LENNY *and* TEDDY *are still.*
JOEY *slowly stands. He is close to* RUTH. *He turns from*
RUTH, *looks round at* MAX.
SAM *clutches his head.*
MAX *breathes heavily, very slowly gets to his feet.*
JOEY *moves to him.*
They look at each other.
Silence.
MAX *moves past* JOEY, *walks towards* RUTH. *He gestures
with his stick.*

MAX. Miss.

> RUTH *walks towards him.*

RUTH. Yes?

> *He looks at her.*

MAX. You a mother?
RUTH. Yes.
MAX. How many you got?
RUTH. Three.

> *He turns to* TEDDY.

MAX. All yours, Ted?

> *Pause.*

Teddy, why don't we have a nice cuddle and kiss, eh? Like
the old days? What about a nice cuddle and kiss, eh?
TEDDY. Come on, then.

> *Pause.*

MAX. You want to kiss your old father? Want a cuddle with
your old father?

TEDDY. Come on, then.

TEDDY moves a step towards him.

Come on.

Pause.

MAX. You still love your old Dad, eh?

They face each other.

TEDDY. Come on, Dad. I'm ready for the cuddle.

MAX begins to chuckle, gurgling.
He turns to the family and addresses them.

MAX. He still loves his father!

Curtain

Act Two

Afternoon.

 MAX, TEDDY, LENNY *and* SAM *are about the stage, lighting cigars.*

 JOEY *comes in from* U.L. *with a coffee tray, followed by* RUTH. *He puts the tray down.* RUTH *hands coffee to all the men. She sits with her cup.* MAX *smiles at her.*

RUTH. That was a very good lunch.
MAX. I'm glad you liked it. (*To the others.*) Did you hear that? (*To* RUTH.) Well, I put my heart and soul into it, I can tell you. (*He sips.*) And this is a lovely cup of coffee.
RUTH. I'm glad.
      Pause.
MAX. I've got the feeling you're a first-rate cook.
RUTH. I'm not bad.
MAX. No, I've got the feeling you're a number one cook. Am I right, Teddy?
TEDDY. Yes, she's a very good cook.

      Pause.

MAX. Well, it's a long time since the whole family was together, eh? If only your mother was alive. Eh, what do you say, Sam? What would Jessie say if she was alive? Sitting here with her three sons. Three fine grown-up lads. And a lovely daughter-in-law. The only shame is her grand-children aren't here. She'd have petted them and cooed over them, wouldn't she, Sam? She'd have fussed over them and played with them, told them stories, tickled them – I tell you she'd have been hysterical. (*To* RUTH.) Mind you, she taught those boys everything they know. She taught them

all the morality they know. I'm telling you. Every single bit
of the moral code they live by – was taught to them by their
mother. And she had a heart to go with it. What a heart. Eh,
Sam? Listen, what's the use of beating round the bush?
That woman was the backbone to this family. I mean, I was
busy working twenty-four hours a day in the shop, I was
going all over the country to find meat, I was making my
way in the world, but I left a woman at home with a will of
iron, a heart of gold and a mind. Right, Sam?

Pause.

What a mind.

Pause.

Mind you, I was a generous man to her. I never left her
short of a few bob. I remember one year I entered into
negotiations with a top-class group of butchers with conti-
nental connections. I was going into association with them.
I remember the night I came home, I kept quiet. First of all
I gave Lenny a bath, then Teddy a bath, then Joey a bath.
What fun we used to have in the bath, eh, boys? Then I
came downstairs and I made Jessie put her feet up on a
pouffe – what happened to that pouffe, I haven't seen it for
years – she put her feet up on the pouffe and I said to her,
Jessie, I think our ship is going to come home, I'm going to
treat you to a couple of items, I'm going to buy you a dress in
pale corded blue silk, heavily encrusted in pearls, and for
casual wear, a pair of pantaloons in lilac flowered taffeta.
Then I gave her a drop of cherry brandy. I remember the
boys came down, in their pyjamas, all their hair shining,
their faces pink, it was before they started shaving, and they
knelt down at our feet, Jessie's and mine. I tell you, it was
like Christmas.

Pause.

RUTH. What happened to the group of butchers?

MAX. The group? They turned out to be a bunch of criminals like everyone else.

Pause.

This is a lousy cigar.

He stubs it out.
He turns to SAM.

What time you going to work?

SAM. Soon.

MAX. You've got a job on this afternoon, haven't you?

SAM. Yes, I know.

MAX. What do you mean, you know? You'll be late. You'll lose your job? What are you trying to do, humiliate me?

SAM. Don't worry about me.

MAX. It makes the bile come up in my mouth. The bile – you understand? (*To* RUTH.) I worked as a butcher all my life, using the chopper and the slab, the slab, you know what I mean, the chopper and the slab! To keep my family in luxury. Two families! My mother was bedridden, my brothers were all invalids. I had to earn the money for the leading psychiatrists. I had to read books! I had to study the disease, so that I could cope with an emergency at every stage. A crippled family, three bastard sons, a slutbitch of a wife – don't talk to me about the pain of childbirth – I suffered the pain, I've still got the pangs – when I give a little cough my back collapses – and here I've got a lazy idle bugger of a brother won't even get to work on time. The best chauffeur in the world. All his life he's sat in the front seat giving lovely hand signals. You call that work? This man doesn't know his gearbox from his arse!

SAM. You go and ask my customers! I'm the only one they ever ask for.

MAX. What do the other drivers do, sleep all day?

SAM. I can only drive one car. They can't all have me at the same time.

MAX. Anyone could have you at the same time. You'd bend over for half a dollar on Blackfriars Bridge.

SAM. Me!

MAX. For two bob and a toffee apple.

SAM. He's insulting me. He's insulting his brother. I'm driving a man to Hampton Court at four forty-five.

MAX. Do you want to know who could drive? MacGregor! MacGregor was a driver.

SAM. Don't you believe it.

MAX *points his stick at* SAM.

MAX. He didn't even fight in the war. This man didn't even fight in the bloody war!

SAM. I did!

MAX. Who did you kill?

Silence.

SAM *gets up, goes to* RUTH, *shakes her hand and goes out of the front door.*

MAX *turns to* TEDDY.

Well, how you been keeping, son?

TEDDY. I've been keeping very well, Dad.

MAX. It's nice to have you with us, son.

TEDDY. It's nice to be back, Dad.

Pause.

MAX. You should have told me you were married, Teddy. I'd have sent you a present. Where was the wedding, in America?

TEDDY. No. Here. The day before we left.

MAX. Did you have a big function?

TEDDY. No, there was no one there.

MAX. You're mad. I'd have given you a white wedding. We'd

have had the cream of the cream here. I'd have been only
too glad to bear the expense, my word of honour.

Pause.

TEDDY. You were busy at the time. I didn't want to bother
you.

MAX. But you're my own flesh and blood. You're my first born.
I'd have dropped everything. Sam would have driven you
to the reception in the Snipe, Lenny would have been your
best man, and then we'd have all seen you off on the boat. I
mean, you don't think I disapprove of marriage, do you?
Don't be daft. (*To* RUTH.) I've been begging my two
youngsters for years to find a nice feminine girl with proper
credentials – it makes life worth living. (*To* TEDDY.) Anyway, what's the difference, you did it, you made a wonderful
choice, you've got a wonderful family, a marvellous career
. . . so why don't we let bygones be bygones?

Pause.

You know what I'm saying? I want you both to know that
you have my blessing.

TEDDY. Thank you.

MAX. Don't mention it. How many other houses in the district
have got a Doctor of Philosophy sitting down drinking a cup
of coffee?

Pause.

RUTH. I'm sure Teddy's very happy . . . to know that you're
pleased with me.

Pause.

I think he wondered whether you would be pleased with me.

MAX. But you're a charming woman.

Pause.

RUTH. I was . . .
MAX. What?

Pause.

What she say?

They all look at her.

RUTH. I was . . . different . . . when I met Teddy . . .
first.
TEDDY. No you weren't. You were the same.
RUTH. I wasn't.
MAX. Who cares? Listen, live in the present, what are you
worrying about? I mean, don't forget the earth's about
five thousand million years old, at least. Who can afford to
live in the past?

Pause.

TEDDY. She's a great help to me over there. She's a wonderful
wife and mother. She's a very popular woman. She's got
lots of friends. It's a great life, at the University . . . you
know . . . it's a very good life. We've got a lovely house
. . . we've got all . . . we've got everything we want. It's
a very stimulating environment.

Pause.

My department . . . is highly successful.

Pause.

We've got three boys, you know.
MAX. All boys? Isn't that funny, eh? You've got three, I've
got three. You've got three nephews, Joey. Joey! You're an
uncle, do you hear? You could teach them how to box.

Pause.

JOEY (*to* RUTH). I'm a boxer. In the evenings, after work. I'm in demolition in the daytime.

RUTH. Oh?

JOEY. Yes. I hope to be full time, when I get more bouts.

MAX (*to* LENNY). He speaks so easily to his sister-in-law, do you notice? That's because she's an intelligent and sympathetic woman.

He leans to her.

Eh, tell me, do you think the children are missing their mother?

She looks at him.

TEDDY. Of course they are. They love her. We'll be seeing them soon.

Pause.

LENNY (*to* TEDDY). Your cigar's gone out.

TEDDY. Oh, yes.

LENNY. Want a light?

TEDDY. No. No.

Pause.

So has yours.

LENNY. Oh, yes.

Pause.

Eh, Teddy, you haven't told us much about your Doctorship of Philosophy. What do you teach?

TEDDY. Philosophy.

LENNY. Well, I want to ask you something. Do you detect a certain logical incoherence in the central affirmations of Christian theism?

TEDDY. That question doesn't fall within my province.

LENNY. Well, look at it this way . . . you don't mind my asking you some questions, do you?

TEDDY. If they're within my province.

LENNY. Well, look at it this way. How can the unknown merit reverence? In other words, how can you revere that of which you're ignorant? At the same time, it would be ridiculous to propose that what we *know* merits reverence. What we know merits any one of a number of things, but it stands to reason reverence isn't one of them. In other words, apart from the known and the unknown, what else is there?

Pause.

TEDDY. I'm afraid I'm the wrong person to ask.

LENNY. But you're a philosopher. Come on, be frank. What do you make of all this business of being and not-being?

TEDDY. What do you make of it?

LENNY. Well, for instance, take a table. Philosophically speaking. What is it?

TEDDY. A table.

LENNY. Ah. You mean it's nothing else but a table. Well, some people would envy your certainty, wouldn't they, Joey? For instance, I've got a couple of friends of mine, we often sit round the Ritz Bar having a few liqueurs, and they're always saying things like that, you know, things like: Take a table, take it. All right, I say, *take* it, *take* a table, but once you've taken it, what you going to do with it? Once you've got hold of it, where you going to take it?

MAX. You'd probably sell it.

LENNY. You wouldn't get much for it.

JOEY. Chop it up for firewood.

LENNY *looks at him and laughs.*

RUTH. Don't be too sure though. You've forgotten something. Look at me. I . . . move my leg. That's all it is. But I wear . . . underwear . . . which moves with me . . . it

. . . captures your attention. Perhaps you misinterpret. The action is simple. It's a leg . . . moving. My lips move. Why don't you restrict . . . your observations to that? Perhaps the fact that they move is more significant . . . than the words which come through them. You must bear that . . . possibility . . . in mind.

Silence.
TEDDY *stands.*

I was born quite near here.

Pause.

Then . . . six years ago, I went to America.

Pause.

It's all rock. And sand. It stretches . . . so far . . . everywhere you look. And there's lots of insects there.

Pause.

And there's lots of insects there.

Silence.
She is still.
MAX *stands.*

MAX. Well, it's time to go to the gym. Time for your workout, Joey.

LENNY (*standing*). I'll come with you.

JOEY *sits looking at* RUTH.

MAX. Joe.

JOEY *stands. The three go out.*
TEDDY *sits by* RUTH, *holds her hand.*
She smiles at him.
Pause.

TEDDY. I think we'll go back. Mmnn ?

Pause.

Shall we go home ?

RUTH. Why ?

TEDDY. Well, we were only here for a few days, weren't we ?
We might as well . . . cut it short, I think.

RUTH. Why ? Don't you like it here ?

TEDDY. Of course I do. But I'd like to go back and see the
boys now.

Pause.

RUTH. Don't you like your family ?

TEDDY. Which family ?

RUTH. Your family here.

TEDDY. Of course I like them. What are you talking about ?

Pause.

RUTH. You don't like them as much as you thought you did ?

TEDDY. Of course I do. Of course I . . . like them. I don't
know what you're talking about.

Pause.

Listen. You know what time of the day it is there now, do
you ?

RUTH. What ?

TEDDY. It's morning. It's about eleven o'clock.

RUTH. Is it ?

TEDDY. Yes, they're about six hours behind us . . . I mean
. . . behind the time here. The boys'll be at the pool . . .
now . . . swimming. Think of it. Morning over there. Sun.
We'll go anyway, mmnn ? It's so clean there.

RUTH. Clean.

TEDDY. Yes.

RUTH. Is it dirty here ?

TEDDY. No, of course not. But it's cleaner there.

Pause.

Look, I just brought you back to meet the family, didn't I? You've met them, we can go. The fall semester will be starting soon.

RUTH. You find it dirty here?

TEDDY. I didn't say I found it dirty here.

Pause.

I didn't say that.

Pause.

Look. I'll go and pack. You rest for a while. Will you? They won't be back for at least an hour. You can sleep. Rest. Please.

She looks at him.

You can help me with my lectures when we get back. I'd love that. I'd be so grateful for it, really. We can bathe till October. You know that. Here, there's nowhere to bathe, except the swimming bath down the road. You know what it's like? It's like a urinal. A filthy urinal!

Pause.

You liked Venice, didn't you? It was lovely, wasn't it? You had a good week. I mean . . . I took you there. I can speak Italian.

RUTH. But if I'd been a nurse in the Italian campaign I would have been there before.

Pause.

TEDDY. You just rest. I'll go and pack.

TEDDY goes out and up the stairs.

She closes her eyes.
LENNY appears from U.L.
He walks into the room and sits near her.
She opens her eyes.
Silence.

LENNY. Well, the evenings are drawing in.
RUTH. Yes, it's getting dark.

Pause.

LENNY. Winter'll soon be upon us. Time to renew one's wardrobe.

Pause.

RUTH. That's a good thing to do.
LENNY. What?

Pause.

RUTH. I always . . .

Pause.

Do you like clothes?
LENNY. Oh, yes. Very fond of clothes.

Pause.

RUTH. I'm fond . . .

Pause.

What do you think of my shoes?
LENNY. They're very nice.
RUTH. No, I can't get the ones I want over there.
LENNY. Can't get them over there, eh?
RUTH. No . . . you don't get them there.

Pause.

I was a model before I went away.

LENNY. Hats?

Pause.

I bought a girl a hat once. We saw it in a glass case, in a shop. I tell you what it had. It had a bunch of daffodils on it, tied with a black satin bow, and then it was covered with a cloche of black veiling. A cloche. I'm telling you. She was made for it.

RUTH. No . . . I was a model for the body. A photographic model for the body.

LENNY. Indoor work?

RUTH. That was before I had . . . all my children.

Pause.

No, not always indoors.

Pause.

Once or twice we went to a place in the country, by train. Oh, six or seven times. We used to pass a . . . a large white water tower. This place . . . this house . . . was very big . . . the trees . . . there was a lake, you see . . . we used to change and walk down towards the lake . . . we went down a path . . . on stones . . . there were . . . on this path. Oh, just . . . wait . . . yes . . . when we changed in the house we had a drink. There was a cold buffet.

Pause.

Sometimes we stayed in the house but . . . most often . . . we walked down to the lake . . . and did our modelling there.

Pause.

Just before we went to America I went down there. I walked

from the station to the gate and then I walked up the drive. There were lights on . . . I stood in the drive . . . the house was very light.

> TEDDY *comes down the stairs with the cases. He puts them down, looks at* LENNY.

TEDDY. What have you been saying to her?

> *He goes to* RUTH.

Here's your coat.

> LENNY *goes to the radiogram and puts on a record of slow jazz.*

Ruth. Come on. Put it on.

LENNY (*to* RUTH). What about one dance before you go?

TEDDY. We're going.

LENNY. Just one.

TEDDY. No. We're going.

LENNY. Just one dance, with her brother-in-law, before she goes.

> LENNY *bends to her.*

Madam?

> RUTH *stands. They dance, slowly.*
> TEDDY *stands, with* RUTH'S *coat.*
> MAX *and* JOEY *come in the front door and into the room. They stand.*
> LENNY *kisses* RUTH. *They stand, kissing.*

JOEY. Christ, she's wide open. Dad, look at that.

> *Pause.*

She's a tart.

> *Pause.*

Old Lenny's got a tart in here.

JOEY *goes to them. He takes* RUTH'S *arm. He smiles at* LENNY. *He sits with* RUTH *on the sofa, embraces and kisses her.*
He looks up at LENNY.

Just up my street.

He leans her back until she lies beneath him. He kisses her.
He looks up at TEDDY *and* MAX.

It's better than a rubdown, this.

LENNY *sits on the arm of the sofa. He caresses* RUTH'S *hair as* JOEY *embraces her.*
MAX *comes forward, looks at the cases.*

MAX. You going, Teddy? Already?

Pause.

Well, when you coming over again, eh? Look, next time you come over, don't forget to let us know beforehand whether you're married or not. I'll always be glad to meet the wife. Honest. I'm telling you.

JOEY *lies heavily on* RUTH.
They are almost still.
LENNY *caresses her hair.*

Listen, you think I don't know why you didn't tell me you were married? I know why. You were ashamed. You thought I'd be annoyed because you married a woman beneath you. You should have known me better. I'm broadminded. I'm a broadminded man.

He peers to see RUTH'S *face under* JOEY, *turns back to* TEDDY.

Mind you, she's a lovely girl. A beautiful woman. And a

mother too. A mother of three. You've made a happy woman out of her. It's something to be proud of. I mean, we're talking about a woman of quality. We're talking about a woman of feeling.

> JOEY *and* RUTH *roll off the sofa on to the floor.*
> JOEY *clasps her.* LENNY *moves to stand above them. He looks down on them. He touches* RUTH *gently with his foot.*
> RUTH *suddenly pushes* JOEY *away.*
> *She stands up.*
> JOEY *gets to his feet, stares at her.*

RUTH. I'd like something to eat. (*To* LENNY.) I'd like a drink. Did you get any drink?
LENNY. We've got drink.
RUTH. I'd like one, please.
LENNY. What drink?
RUTH. Whisky.
LENNY. I've got it.

> *Pause.*

RUTH. Well, get it.

> LENNY *goes to the sideboard, takes out bottle and glasses.*
> JOEY *moves towards her.*

Put the record off.

> *He looks at her, turns, puts the record off.*

I want something to eat.

> *Pause.*

JOEY. I can't cook. (*Pointing to* MAX.) He's the cook.

> LENNY *brings her a glass of whisky.*

LENNY. Soda on the side?
RUTH. What's this glass? I can't drink out of this. Haven't you got a tumbler?

LENNY. Yes.

RUTH. Well, put it in a tumbler.

He takes the glass back, pours whisky into a tumbler, brings it to her.

LENNY. On the rocks? Or as it comes?

RUTH. Rocks? What do you know about rocks?

LENNY. We've got rocks. But they're frozen stiff in the fridge.

RUTH drinks.
LENNY looks round at the others.

Drinks all round?

He goes to the sideboard and pours drinks.
JOEY moves closer to RUTH.

JOEY. What food do you want?

RUTH walks round the room.

RUTH (*to* TEDDY). Have your family read your critical works?

MAX. That's one thing I've never done. I've never read one of his critical works.

TEDDY. You wouldn't understand them.

LENNY hands drinks all round.

JOEY. What sort of food do you want? I'm not the cook, anyway.

LENNY. Soda, Ted? Or as it comes?

TEDDY. You wouldn't understand my works. You wouldn't have the faintest idea of what they were about. You wouldn't appreciate the points of reference. You're way behind. All of you. There's no point in my sending you my works. You'd be lost. It's nothing to do with the question of intelligence. It's a way of being able to look at the world. It's a question of how far you can operate on things and not in things. I mean it's a question of your capacity to ally the two, to relate the two, to balance the two. To see, to be able to *see*! I'm the one who can see. That's why I can write my critical works. Might do you good . . . have a look at them . . . see how certain people can view . . . things . . . how certain people can maintain . . . intellectual equilibrium. Intellectual equilibrium. You're just objects. You just . . . move about. I can observe it. I can see what you do. It's the same as I do. But you're lost in it. You won't get me being . . . I won't be lost in it.

BLACKOUT.
LIGHTS UP.
Evening.
TEDDY *sitting, in his coat, the cases by him.* SAM.
Pause.

SAM. Do you remember MacGregor, Teddy?
TEDDY. Mac?
SAM. Yes.
TEDDY. Of course I do.
SAM. What did you think of him? Did you take to him?
TEDDY. Yes. I liked him. Why?

Pause.

SAM. You know, you were always my favourite, of the lads. Always.

Pause.

When you wrote to me from America I was very touched, you know. I mean you'd written to your father a few times but you'd never written to me. But then, when I got that letter from you . . . well, I was very touched. I never told him. I never told him I'd heard from you.

Pause.

(*Whispering.*) Teddy, shall I tell you something? You were always your mother's favourite. She told me. It's true. You were always the . . . you were always the main object of her love.

Pause.

Why don't you stay for a couple more weeks, eh? We could have a few laughs.

LENNY *comes in the front door and into the room.*

LENNY. Still here, Ted? You'll be late for your first seminar.

He goes to the sideboard, opens it, peers in it, to the right and the left, stands.

Where's my cheese-roll?

Pause.

Someone's taken my cheese-roll. I left it there. (*To* SAM.) You been thieving?

TEDDY. I took your cheese-roll, Lenny.

Silence.
SAM *looks at them, picks up his hat and goes out of the front door.*
Silence.

LENNY. You took my cheese-roll?
TEDDY. Yes.
LENNY. I made that roll myself. I cut it and put the butter on. I sliced a piece of cheese and put it in between. I put it on a plate and I put it in the sideboard. I did all that before I went out. Now I come back and you've eaten it.
TEDDY. Well, what are you going to do about it?
LENNY. I'm waiting for you to apologize.
TEDDY. But I took it deliberately, Lenny.

LENNY. You mean you didn't stumble on it by mistake?

TEDDY. No, I saw you put it there. I was hungry, so I ate it.

Pause.

LENNY. Barefaced audacity.

Pause.

What led you to be so . . . vindictive against your own brother? I'm bowled over.

Pause.

Well, Ted, I would say this is something approaching the naked truth, isn't it? It's a real cards on the table stunt. I mean, we're in the land of no holds barred now. Well, how else can you interpret it? To pinch your younger brother's specially made cheese-roll when he's out doing a spot of work, that's not equivocal, it's unequivocal.

Pause.

Mind you, I will say you do seem to have grown a bit sulky during the last six years. A bit sulky. A bit inner. A bit less forthcoming. It's funny, because I'd have thought that in the United States of America, I mean with the sun and all that, the open spaces, on the old campus, in your position, lecturing, in the centre of all the intellectual life out there, on the old campus, all the social whirl, all the stimulation of it all, all your kids and all that, to have fun with, down by the pool, the Greyhound buses and all that, tons of iced water, all the comfort of those Bermuda shorts and all that, on the old campus, no time of the day or night you can't get a cup of coffee or a Dutch gin, I'd have thought you'd have grown more forthcoming, not less. Because I want you to know that you set a standard for us, Teddy. Your family looks up to you, boy, and you know what it does? It does its best to follow the example you set. Because you're a great source of pride to us. That's why we were so glad to see you come back, to welcome you back to your birthplace. That's why.

Pause.

No, listen, Ted, there's no question that we live a less rich life here than you do over there. We live a closer life. We're busy, of course. Joey's busy with his boxing, I'm busy with my occupation, Dad still plays a good game of poker, and he does the cooking as well, well up to his old standard, and Uncle Sam's the best chauffeur in the firm. But nevertheless we do make up a unit, Teddy, and you're an integral part of it. When we all sit round the backyard having a quiet gander at the night sky, there's always an empty chair standing in the circle, which is in fact yours. And so when you at length return to us, we do expect a bit of grace, a bit of je ne sais quoi, a bit of generosity of mind, a bit of liberality of spirit, to reassure us. We do expect that. But do we get it? Have we got it? Is that what you've given us?

Pause.

TEDDY. Yes.

JOEY *comes down the stairs and into the room, with a newspaper.*

LENNY (*to* JOEY). How'd you get on?
JOEY. Er . . . not bad.
LENNY. What do you mean?

Pause.

What do you mean?
JOEY. Not bad.
LENNY. I want to know what you *mean* – by not bad.
JOEY. What's it got to do with you?
LENNY. Joey, you tell your brother everything.

Pause.

JOEY. I didn't get all the way.
LENNY. You didn't get all the way?

Pause.

(*With emphasis.*) You didn't get all the way?
But you've had her up there for two hours.
JOEY. Well?
LENNY. You didn't get all the way and you've had her up there
for two hours!
JOEY. What about it?

LENNY *moves closer to him.*

LENNY. What are you telling me?
JOEY. What do you mean?
LENNY. Are you telling me she's a tease?

Pause.

She's a tease!

Pause.

What do you think of that, Ted? Your wife turns out to be
a tease. He's had her up there for two hours and he didn't
go the whole hog.
JOEY. I didn't say she was a tease.
LENNY. Are you joking? It sounds like a tease to me, don't it
to you, Ted?
TEDDY. Perhaps he hasn't got the right touch.
LENNY. Joey? Not the right touch? Don't be ridiculous. He's
had more dolly than you've had cream cakes. He's irresistible.
He's one of the few and far between. Tell him about the
last bird you had, Joey.

Pause.

JOEY. What bird?

LENNY. The last bird! When we stopped the car . . .

JOEY. Oh, that . . . yes . . . well, we were in Lenny's car one night last week . . .

LENNY. The Alfa.

JOEY. And er . . . bowling down the road . . .

LENNY. Up near the Scrubs.

JOEY. Yes, up over by the Scrubs . . .

LENNY. We were doing a little survey of North Paddington.

JOEY. And er . . . it was pretty late, wasn't it?

LENNY. Yes, it was late. Well?

Pause.

JOEY. And then we . . . well, by the kerb, we saw this parked car . . . with a couple of girls in it.

LENNY. And their escorts.

JOEY. Yes, there were two geezers in it. Anyway . . .

Pause.

What we do then?

LENNY. We stopped the car and got out!

JOEY. Yes . . . we got out . . . and we told the . . . two escorts . . . to go away . . . which they did . . . and then we . . . got the girls out of the car . . .

LENNY. We didn't take them over the Scrubs.

JOEY. Oh, no. Not over the Scrubs. Well, the police would have noticed us there . . . you see. We took them over a bombed site.

LENNY. Rubble. In the rubble.

JOEY. Yes, plenty of rubble.

Pause.

Well . . . you know . . . then we had them.

LENNY. You've missed out the best bit. He's missed out the best bit!

JOEY. What bit?

LENNY (*to* TEDDY). His bird says to him, I don't mind, she says, but I've got to have some protection. I've got to have some contraceptive protection. I haven't got any contraceptive protection, old Joey says to her. In that case I won't do it, she says. Yes you will, says Joey, never mind about the contraceptive protection.

　　LENNY *laughs*.

Even my bird laughed when she heard that. Yes, even she gave out a bit of a laugh. So you can't say old Joey isn't a bit of a knockout when he gets going, can you? And here he is upstairs with your wife for two hours and he hasn't even been the whole hog. Well, your wife sounds like a bit of a tease to me, Ted. What do you make of it, Joey? You satisfied? Don't tell me you're satisfied without going the whole hog?

　　Pause.

JOEY. I've been the whole hog plenty of times. Sometimes . . . you can be happy . . . and not go the whole hog. Now and again . . . you can be happy . . . without going any hog.

　　LENNY *stares at him*.
　　MAX *and* SAM *come in the front door and into the room*.

MAX. Where's the whore? Still in bed? She'll make us all animals.
LENNY. The girl's a tease.
MAX. What?
LENNY. She's had Joey on a string.
MAX. What do you mean?
TEDDY. He had her up there for two hours and he didn't go the whole hog.

　　Pause.

MAX. My Joey? She did that to my boy?

Pause.

To my youngest son? Tch, tch, tch, tch. How you feeling, son? Are you all right?

JOEY. Sure I'm all right.

MAX (*to* TEDDY). Does she do that to you, too?

TEDDY. No.

LENNY. He gets the gravy.

MAX. You think so?

JOEY. No he don't.

Pause.

SAM. He's her lawful husband. She's his lawful wife.

JOEY. No he don't! He don't get no gravy! I'm telling you. I'm telling all of you. I'll kill the next man who says he gets the gravy.

MAX. Joey . . . what are you getting so excited about? (*To* LENNY.) It's because he's frustrated. You see what happens?

JOEY. Who is?

MAX. Joey. No one's saying you're wrong. In fact everyone's saying you're right.

Pause.
MAX *turns to the others.*

You know something? Perhaps it's not a bad idea to have a woman in the house. Perhaps it's a good thing. Who knows? Maybe we should keep her.

Pause.

Maybe we'll ask her if she wants to stay.

Pause.

TEDDY. I'm afraid not, Dad. She's not well, and we've got to get home to the children.

MAX. Not well? I told you, I'm used to looking after people

who are not so well. Don't worry about that. Perhaps we'll
keep her here.

Pause.

SAM. Don't be silly.
MAX. What's silly?
SAM. You're talking rubbish.
MAX. Me?
SAM. She's got three children.
MAX. She can have more! Here. If she's so keen.
TEDDY. She doesn't want any more.
MAX. What do you know about what she wants, eh, Ted?
TEDDY (*smiling*). The best thing for her is to come home with
me, Dad. Really. We're married, you know.

MAX *walks about the room, clicks his fingers.*

MAX. We'd have to pay her, of course. You realize that? We
can't leave her walking about without any pocket money.
She'll have to have a little allowance.
JOEY. Of course we'll pay her. She's got to have some money
in her pocket.
MAX. That's what I'm saying. You can't expect a woman to
walk about without a few bob to spend on a pair of stockings.

Pause.

LENNY. Where's the money going to come from?
MAX. Well, how much is she worth? What we talking about,
three figures?
LENNY. I asked you where the money's going to come from.
It'll be an extra mouth to feed. It'll be an extra body to
clothe. You realize that?
JOEY. I'll buy her clothes.
LENNY. What with?
JOEY. I'll put in a certain amount out of my wages.
MAX. That's it. We'll pass the hat round. We'll make a

donation. We're all grown-up people, we've got a sense of responsibility. We'll all put a little in the hat. It's democratic.

LENNY. It'll come to a few quid, Dad.

Pause.

I mean, she's not a woman who likes walking around in second-hand goods. She's up to the latest fashion. You wouldn't want her walking about in clothes which don't show her off at her best, would you?

MAX. Lenny, do you mind if I make a little comment? It's not meant to be critical. But I think you're concentrating too much on the economic considerations. There are other considerations. There are the human considerations. You understand what I mean? There are the human considerations. Don't forget them.

LENNY. I won't.

MAX. Well don't.

Pause.

Listen, we're bound to treat her in something approximating, at least, to the manner in which she's accustomed. After all, she's not someone off the street, she's my daughter-in-law!

JOEY. That's right.

MAX. There you are, you see. Joey'll donate, Sam'll donate. . . .

SAM *looks at him.*

I'll put in a few bob out of my pension, Lenny'll cough up. We're laughing. What about you, Ted? How much you going to put in the kitty?

TEDDY. I'm not putting anything in the kitty.

MAX. What? You won't even help to support your own wife? I thought he was a son of mine. You lousy stinkpig. Your mother would drop dead if she heard you take that attitude.

LENNY. Eh, Dad.

LENNY walks forward.

I've got a better idea.

MAX. What?

LENNY. There's no need for us to go to all this expense. I know these women. Once they get started they ruin your budget. I've got a better idea. Why don't I take her up with me to Greek Street?

Pause.

MAX. You mean put her on the game?

Pause.

We'll put her on the game. That's a stroke of genius, that's a marvellous idea. You mean she can earn the money herself – on her back?

LENNY. Yes.

MAX. Wonderful. The only thing is, it'll have to be short hours. We don't want her out of the house all night.

LENNY. I can limit the hours.

MAX. How many?

LENNY. Four hours a night.

MAX (*dubiously*). Is that enough?

LENNY. She'll bring in a good sum for four hours a night.

MAX. Well, you should know. After all, it's true, the last thing we want to do is wear the girl out. She's going to have her obligations this end as well. Where you going to put her in Greek Street?

LENNY. It doesn't have to be right in Greek Street, Dad. I've got a number of flats all around that area.

MAX. You have? Well, what about me? Why don't you give me one?

LENNY. You're sexless.

JOEY. Eh, wait a minute, what's all this?

MAX. I know what Lenny's saying. Lenny's saying she can pay her own way. What do you think, Teddy? That'll solve all our problems.

JOEY. Eh, wait a minute. I don't want to share her.

MAX. What did you say?

JOEY. I don't want to share her with a lot of yobs!

MAX. Yobs! You arrogant git! What arrogance. (*To* LENNY.) Will you be supplying her with yobs?

LENNY. I've got a very distinguished clientèle, Joey. They're more distinguished than you'll ever be.

MAX. So you can count yourself lucky we're including you in.

JOEY. I didn't think I was going to have to share her!

MAX. Well, you *are* going to have to share her! Otherwise she goes straight back to America. You understand?

Pause.

It's tricky enough as it is, without you shoving your oar in. But there's something worrying me. Perhaps she's not so up to the mark. Eh? Teddy, you're the best judge. Do you think she'd be up to the mark?

Pause.

I mean what about all this teasing? Is she going to make a habit of it? That'll get us nowhere.

Pause.

TEDDY. It was just love play . . . I suppose . . . that's all I suppose it was.

MAX. Love play? Two bleeding hours? That's a bloody long time for love play!

LENNY. I don't think we've got anything to worry about on that score, Dad.

MAX. How do you know?

LENNY. I'm giving you a professional opinion.

LENNY *goes to* TEDDY.

LENNY. Listen, Teddy, you could help us, actually. If I were to send you some cards, over to America . . . you know, very nice ones, with a name on, and a telephone number, very discreet, well, you could distribute them . . . to various parties, who might be making a trip over here. Of course, you'd get a little percentage out of it.

MAX. I mean, you needn't tell them she's your wife.

LENNY. No, we'd call her something else. Dolores, or something.

MAX. Or Spanish Jacky.

LENNY. No, you've got to be reserved about it, Dad. We could call her something nice . . . like Cynthia . . . or Gillian.

Pause.

JOEY. Gillian.

Pause.

LENNY. No, what I mean, Teddy, you must know lots of professors, heads of departments, men like that. They pop over here for a week at the Savoy, they need somewhere they can go to have a nice quiet poke. And of course you'd be in a position to give them inside information.

MAX. Sure. You can give them proper data. You know, the kind of thing she's willing to do. How far she'd be prepared to go with their little whims and fancies. Eh, Lenny? To what extent she's various. I mean if you don't know who does?

Pause.

I bet you before two months we'd have a waiting list.

LENNY. You could be our representative in the States.

MAX. Of course. We're talking in international terms! By the time we've finished Pan-American'll give us a discount.

Pause.

TEDDY. She'd get old . . . very quickly.

MAX. No . . . not in this day and age! With the health service? Old! How could she get old? She'll have the time of her life.

> RUTH *comes down the stairs, dressed.*
> *She comes into the room.*
> *She smiles at the gathering, and sits.*
> *Silence.*

TEDDY. Ruth . . . the family have invited you to stay, for a little while longer. As a . . . as a kind of guest. If you like the idea I don't mind. We can manage very easily at home . . . until you come back.

RUTH. How very nice of them.

> *Pause.*

MAX. It's an offer from our heart.

RUTH. It's very sweet of you.

MAX. Listen . . . it would be our pleasure.

> *Pause.*

RUTH. I think I'd be too much trouble.

MAX. Trouble? What are you talking about? What trouble? Listen, I'll tell you something. Since poor Jessie died, eh, Sam? we haven't had a woman in the house. Not one. Inside this house. And I'll tell you why. Because their mother's image was so dear any other woman would have . . . tarnished it. But you . . . Ruth . . . you're not only lovely and beautiful, but you're kin. You're kith. You belong here.

> *Pause.*

RUTH. I'm very touched.

MAX. Of course you're touched. I'm touched.

Pause.

TEDDY. But Ruth, I should tell you . . . that you'll have to pull your weight a little, if you stay. Financially. My father isn't very well off.

RUTH (*to* MAX). Oh, I'm sorry.

MAX. No, you'd just have to bring in a little, that's all. A few pennies. Nothing much. It's just that we're waiting for Joey to hit the top as a boxer. When Joey hits the top . . . well . . .

Pause.

TEDDY. Or you can come home with me.

LENNY. We'd get you a flat.

Pause.

RUTH. A flat?

LENNY. Yes.

RUTH. Where?

LENNY. In town.

Pause.

But you'd live here, with us.

MAX. Of course you would. This would be your home. In the bosom of the family.

LENNY. You'd just pop up to the flat a couple of hours a night, that's all.

MAX. Just a couple of hours, that's all. That's all.

LENNY. And you make enough money to keep you going here.

Pause.

RUTH. How many rooms would this flat have?

LENNY. Not many.

RUTH. I would want at least three rooms and a bathroom.

LENNY. You wouldn't need three rooms and a bathroom.

MAX. She'd need a bathroom.

LENNY. But not three rooms.

Pause.

RUTH. Oh, I would. Really.

LENNY. Two would do.

RUTH. No. Two wouldn't be enough.

Pause.

I'd want a dressing-room, a rest-room, and a bedroom.

Pause.

LENNY. All right, we'll get you a flat with three rooms and a bathroom.

RUTH. With what kind of conveniences?

LENNY. All conveniences.

RUTH. A personal maid?

LENNY. Of course.

Pause.

We'd finance you, to begin with, and then, when you were established, you could pay us back, in instalments.

RUTH. Oh, no, I wouldn't agree to that.

LENNY. Oh, why not?

RUTH. You would have to regard your original outlay simply as a capital investment.

Pause.

LENNY. I see. All right.

RUTH. You'd supply my wardrobe, of course?

LENNY. We'd supply everything. Everything you need.

RUTH. I'd need an awful lot. Otherwise I wouldn't be content.

LENNY. You'd have everything.

RUTH. I would naturally want to draw up an inventory of everything I would need, which would require your signatures in the presence of witnesses.

LENNY. Naturally.

RUTH. All aspects of the agreement and conditions of employment would have to be clarified to our mutual satisfaction before we finalized the contract.

LENNY. Of course.

Pause.

RUTH. Well, it might prove a workable arrangement.

LENNY. I think so.

MAX. And you'd have the whole of your daytime free, of course. You could do a bit of cooking here if you wanted to.

LENNY. Make the beds.

MAX. Scrub the place out a bit.

TEDDY. Keep everyone company.

SAM *comes forward.*

SAM (*in one breath*). MacGregor had Jessie in the back of my cab as I drove them along.

He croaks and collapses.
He lies still.
They look at him.

MAX. What's he done? Dropped dead?

LENNY. Yes.

MAX. A corpse? A corpse on my floor? Get him out of here! Clear him out of here!

JOEY *bends over* SAM.

JOEY. He's not dead.

LENNY. He probably was dead, for about thirty seconds.

MAX. He's not even dead!

LENNY *looks down at* SAM.

LENNY. Yes, there's still some breath there.

MAX (*pointing at* SAM). You know what that man had?

LENNY. Has.

MAX. Has! A diseased imagination.

Pause.

RUTH. Yes, it sounds a very attractive idea.

MAX. Do you want to shake on it now, or do you want to leave it till later?

RUTH. Oh, we'll leave it till later.

> TEDDY *stands.*
> *He looks down at* SAM.

TEDDY. I was going to ask him to drive me to London Airport.

> *He goes to the cases, picks one up.*

Well, I'll leave your case, Ruth. I'll just go up the road to the Underground.

MAX. Listen, if you go the other way, first left, first right, you remember, you might find a cab passing there.

TEDDY. Yes, I might do that.

MAX. Or you can take the tube to Piccadilly Circus, won't take you ten minutes, and pick up a cab from there out to the Airport.

TEDDY. Yes, I'll probably do that.

MAX. Mind you, they'll charge you double fare. They'll charge you for the return trip. It's over the six-mile limit.

TEDDY. Yes. Well, bye-bye, Dad. Look after yourself.

> *They shake hands.*

MAX. Thanks, son. Listen. I want to tell you something. It's been wonderful to see you.

Pause.

TEDDY. It's been wonderful to see you.

MAX. Do your boys know about me? Eh? Would they like to see a photo, do you think, of their grandfather?

TEDDY. I know they would.

MAX *brings out his wallet.*

MAX. I've got one on me. I've got one here. Just a minute.
Here you are. Will they like that one?
TEDDY (*taking it*). They'll be thrilled.

He turns to LENNY.

Good-bye, Lenny.

They shake hands.

LENNY. Ta-ta, Ted. Good to see you. Have a good trip.
TEDDY. Bye-bye, Joey.

JOEY *does not move.*

JOEY. Ta-ta.

TEDDY *goes to the front door.*

RUTH. Eddie.

TEDDY *turns.*

Pause.

Don't become a stranger.

TEDDY *goes, shuts the front door.*
Silence.
The three men stand.
RUTH *sits relaxed in her chair.*
SAM *lies still.*
JOEY *walks slowly across the room.*
He kneels at her chair.
She touches his head, lightly.
He puts his head in her lap.
MAX *begins to move above them, backwards and forwards.*
LENNY *stands still.*
MAX *turns to* LENNY.

MAX. I'm too old, I suppose. She thinks I'm an old man.

Pause.

I'm not such an old man.

Pause.

(*To* RUTH.) You think I'm too old for you?

Pause.

Listen. You think you're just going to get that big slag all
the time? You think you're just going to have him . . .
you're going to just have him all the time? You're going to
have to work! You'll have to take them on, you understand?

Pause.

Does she realize that?

Pause.

Lenny, do you think she understands . . .

He begins to stammer.

What . . . what . . . what . . . we're getting at? What
. . . we've got in mind? Do you think she's got it clear?

Pause.

I don't think she's got it clear.

Pause.

You understand what I mean? Listen, I've got a funny idea
she'll do the dirty on us, you want to bet? She'll use us,
she'll make use of us, I can tell you! I can smell it! You
want to bet?

Pause.

She won't . . . be adaptable!

He falls to his knees, whimpers, begins to moan and sob.
He stops sobbing, crawls past SAM'S *body round her chair,*
to the other side of her.

I'm not an old man.

He looks up at her.

Do you hear me?

He raises his face to her.

Kiss me.

She continues to touch JOEY'S *head, lightly.*
LENNY *stands, watching.*

Curtain